The Handbook

Lessons for My Children

By **Afshin Zarenejad Ph.D.**

TABLE OF CONTENTS

Introduction

I recently had one of those milestone birthdays you get once you reach a certain age. One of the birthdays that makes you wonder if the number of days ahead of you is still more than the number of days behind you. I realized that I had gone through a lot and recently had some noteworthy events that led to much self-reflection. I decided to jot down some thoughts and ideas, even lessons, for my children so that I could pass something to them that might be useful to them as they grow up. I also find myself in situations where I react differently than I should in certain situations. Still, I am good about returning to the situation and thinking about what went wrong and why. The result of this is trying to meet the goal of continuous improvement. The person I look up to the most in this world is my wife, who is also my best friend, and I want to do everything to be the best I can be and strive to give her the husband she deserves.

I have learned many lessons that have taught me how to let go of things and understand the cause and effect of life. Most importantly, I have learned how to put some things in the past, deal with some things in the future, and prioritize what I need to deal with right now. As a result, I have been able to lead a less stressful life in the past few years. Suppose I can follow all my suggestions in this 'handbook", a collection of life lessons and reflections. Life might be easier in that case, and I wanted to share those thoughts.

The Ambulance

It was surprisingly bumpy in the back of the cold ambulance that night in November 2015. I had tubes and wires connected to me, and a paramedic just gave me a pill. They said that in about 10 minutes, I would not have anything to worry about. I had just had a severe panic attack. It was not my first, but it was my worst. I was at my desk at work with our new boss, who was changing everything we had built and worked so hard to put it together. The 24-hour Security Operation Center (SOC) was getting close to midnight. He and I were the only ones there because a staff member called out sick. I am pretty sure they did not want to deal with the new manager.

My heart seemed to be beating faster than I could keep up with. I felt control leaving me and the familiar anxiety setting in. The cold chills and shortness of breath set in, and I thought I was having a heart attack. Goosebumps all over my body seemed to connect and form this shell around me that I could not get out of. The air around me was closing in and suffocating me, and I could not breathe. I felt like I was drowning. It is the scariest feeling I have ever had. Even though I had panic attacks before, I never had anything like this. I honestly thought I was having a heart attack and was about to die. I heard the manager say he called 911 and would call my wife. I was already furious, but that made me even more upset. Something about him reaching out to my wife angered me. The other reason I was mad was because I knew from having other panic attacks that I had lost control. I had let this person make me so upset that I did this to myself. All the other panic attacks had boundaries, and I felt safe knowing that there was a limit to how bad they would get. I did not think this was a panic attack because it had far exceeded those boundaries.

Before long, I was in a daze for a while from whatever medication they gave me, and I had come down for my attack. They put me into a room with a concrete floor and light blue square tile walls, like an empty swimming pool. I would later find out that all of the emergency room beds were occupied, and I was put in an operating room. The room was not cold by temperature but had an eerie feeling. I could not put my finger on it, but I knew I was uncomfortable and felt trapped. Now and then, a nurse would come in, and there was something in their tone about me having a panic attack that made me feel very embarrassed. I would get the feeling from these nurses that I was wasting their time because this was not a legitimate emergency.

I had this feeling of embarrassment before. Several times at work, I had more minor versions of these panic attacks, although people would generally be concerned. As time passed, I imagined the feelings of concern from my coworkers slowly changing into looking down at me. I felt ashamed and weak for not being able to control my feelings. I knew there was nothing to feel ashamed about for anyone in this position, but when it happens, you feel the weight of a thousand eyes on you.

As the years passed, I later learned more about how to deal with panic attacks. I realized that feeling this way just made it worse, and I had to have a better understanding of not only what caused panic attacks but also how to view them. I never went back to that office again after that night. I took some medical leave, and when I was ready, I started working again. They allowed me to work remotely, but the anxiety was still there, and not too long after, I resigned because I just needed to mentally and physically separate myself from that place.

I do not know to this day if all the pills I took during that time were a good thing or a bad thing, but I do know that at that time, I was not able to control my attacks by myself. The pills would help keep me calmer and in a semi-sedated state. Anytime the feelings would arise, I would have to take a pill, or if I felt that I was going to be in a high-pressure situation, I would preemptively take a pill. I would not leave my house for a long time, and then when I did, I would not leave alone. Eventually, I was able to go out on my own. Still, I always had a cocktail of pills with me to help with different situations. Perhaps the pills were a necessary tool at that time. Nevertheless, the most important thing I ever did was to go out and study panic attacks, their triggers, and how to prevent them from happening. It has been many years now since the last time I took any of these pills, and I have to say that I am in a far better mental place than I have ever been.

I don't believe that having panic attacks is something that is generally accepted, even in today's day and age. We're more open to issues than we have been in the past, and I may be wrong, but I still feel that people who have panic attacks are perceived as being mentally weak. The good news is that there is help for them, and the lessons I've learned are beneficial to averting panic attacks and generally living a better life. So, my mindset and the concepts that make up this handbook were born from panic attacks. It led me to not only solve that issue but also go above and beyond and deal with anxiety and stress. I went further to learn how to live better by seeing the bigger picture and three boxes.

The Three Boxes

    The three-box technique is not uniquely my idea; it is something that I've learned from years of researching and experimenting with existing techniques that could help me. The idea of leaving items in the past, not worrying about the future, and only dealing with current issues has been around for a long time. Many publications by different experts in their field have taken this idea of the past, present, and future concepts and documented it very well. There is a business strategy by Vijay Govindarajan called the three-box solution, where this philosophy is used (Govindarajan, 2016). The Worry Box Technique from Dr. Monica A. Frank looks at worrying as a relationship between the past and the future. This article discusses connections with insomnia, avoidance, pain, relationship conflicts, and other aspects of worrying (Frank, 2011). The National Institute of Health (NIH) has a study called Uncertainty and Anticipation in Anxiety, which delves into how future threats lead to anxiety with a great deal of detail and a framework that furthers the treatment of clinical anxiety. In another article, I learned how the timing of past, present, and future negative events was associated with anxiety and depression (Eysenck et al., 2006). I found these articles and more to help me understand the bigger picture. Although some articles were more specific to my issues, others were beneficial. Using boxes helped me feel like I was putting thoughts in a container. Still, looking at past, present, and future events is certainly not my idea or something I take credit for. It's just a combination of existing ideas that I used to help me, and perhaps it may help others.

The three-boxes technique's primary goal is to categorize problems or stressors and deal with them accordingly. In my opinion, the most important thing to do when implementing the three-box technique is to be calm and honest. This technique won't be very effective if you are stressed or panicked. I prefer using breathing exercises or even meditating to help calm me down. However, you need to think clearly for this to be effective. This technique is predicated on the idea that you typically cannot solve multiple problems with a single solution. You can only solve one problem at a time. Each problem has its solution. It's a one-to-one correlation, and we should not think about trying to solve multiple problems with a single solution. The moment you have multiple problems in your head is when you can't come up with a singular answer, and the downward spiral of panic occurs again. For example, suppose you are going to a friend's house for dinner. You know a person is attending who you do not get along with. You can't find anything to wear and are running late. You get a call, and your friend asks you to bring a bottle of wine. You're already frantic, and now you must see if you have a bottle of wine and worry if it's decent, and you keep thinking about the person you don't like being there and what snide comment they'll make. Just then, you hear thunder, and it begins to rain.

These are four separate issues, but because they all seem to need to be addressed, they are seen as one big problem. Getting dressed and getting a bottle of wine are two separate issues you can resolve. You can't do anything about the rain, so there is no need to worry about it, and the other person isn't even a problem. You must deal with that situation, which you've probably dealt with multiple times. Keep this idea in mind because for the three boxes to work, you must be calm and able to isolate your problems. This process gives you a sense of control and helps you feel less overwhelmed, empowering you to take charge of your stress and problems.

I have found the three boxes technique to be a very effective way of dealing with issues. It allows me to focus on what I need to worry about, and it often reveals that many things I worry about are not even worth the stress. This realization can make you feel lighter and less burdened, relieving you of unnecessary stress and allowing you to focus on what truly matters. When you get good with this technique, it also helps you prioritize which problems must be addressed first. This technique works because you allow yourself to think of all the issues and problems that are going on in your head.

I like to imagine a conveyor belt, and I start putting everything in my head on this conveyor. The idea behind this is that I'm thinking of everything that is causing anxiety or stress, and I isolate them as individual problems. For example, I might be a bit down because it may be the anniversary of someone who passed away. I may think about that person, and on top of that, I have different tasks to do for my boss. There's an issue with my car, and it's making a weird noise. My coworker makes things very difficult, and my bills have piled up. These are just some examples of things that might be going on in my mind, and it's not uncommon for people to have many more things going on in their minds at any given time. So, once I've begun isolating each issue, each one gets its spot on the conveyor belt.

Identify each item that becomes its item on your mental conveyor belt. I then imagine three boxes in front of me. One of these boxes represents the past, one represents the present, and the other represents the future. I am allowing myself to think of these issues, but I know this is the last time I dwell on them, giving me comfort and reassurance. I think of each item almost like it's coming to me on the conveyor. I think about the problem and decide if it's an event in the past, present, or future. You take that item, and you visualize placing it in that box. Many things in my head or items that occurred in the past belong in that box, or those that have not yet belong in the future box but not in the present box.

Let's say you have a scenario where you're upset because of an argument you may have had with someone in the store. You do not know this person and will probably never see them again, but the event still stews inside you. You are allowing yourself to think about this one last time, and maybe you think about what happened to you and what you would've done differently. Once you take it off the conveyor belt and put it in the box for the past, you're telling yourself that this event is over. Wasting time and energy being upset over it and having it be another negative thing in your head is over. This is just another example of letting go. As each item comes across your mental conveyor belt, you think, is this something that happened in the past that is over and done with, and if so, you put it in the past box. Then, I like to look at the items that are for the future. These are relatively easy because the event has not happened yet. You are worrying about something that hasn't happened yet. Suppose you think about it in many situations like this. Something may resolve that issue altogether or significantly lessen its severity when you worry about a future event. It winds up being a much less straightforward problem. Items that occur in the future are interesting because you must allow yourself to become a procrastinator. Procrastinating has a negative connotation because it means you'll deal with things later, but in this scenario, it is correct. Because you must deal with the problem when it occurs, you can't deal with it in the future state. You don't know exactly the problem or all the parameters around it that could impact how to solve it.

As a kid, I was apprehensive about getting my report card. I had a good idea of what would be on it and how my parents would react, but this philosophy would've allowed me not to worry about it until I got the report card. The result would be the same. In this example of my report card, I still got in trouble with my parents. However, the difference is I wouldn't have made myself sick worrying about it for a week or two ahead of time. However, if you are dealing with something like an issue with your car, worrying about it ahead of time doesn't help. But taking it to the mechanic and letting them come back and tell you what's wrong with it is a step in the right direction. Only then will you have a present problem, which may not be as bad as you thought.

The mechanic will tell you what is wrong with the car, and then you will know your actual problem, not what you may have thought it could be. They'll tell you how to fix the problem with that car and what it will cost. Your future issue has now become a present problem with a solution. The key to a future problem is to wait for it to happen. Until it happens, you're worrying and stressing about something without having all the information. So, you put all the items in your conveyor belt that are future problems in the future box and tell yourself that you will deal with that problem later.

Finally, you have your present box. When I started looking at my items as packages on a conveyor belt, I was struck that I didn't have many present problems. I had a lot of things in the past that caused me to dwell on them, and I was worried about many things in the future, but I didn't have many present problems. Regardless, whatever problem you have right now goes into the present box.

Again, in the beginning, I had a little sheet of paper, and I would write items down on it. Those would go in my present box, and then I look at them and see which is most pressing. Then, I would know which to deal with first, allowing me to prioritize my issues. An exciting realization that comes with this process is not only do you have to separate your stressors from your issues. I see stressors as something we worry about, but there is no solution. You cannot solve past events, and future events haven't happened yet.

You realize that you can only deal with those in your present box. The past box is filled with memories. The future box anticipates events. The present box holds my actual problems. The present box is the only box with issues that can be solved. There's no way to solve dwelling on an issue or worrying about what may happen. One of the exciting things about this technique is the realization that most of your stresses are not issues you must deal with. Use the proper letting go technique for items in your past box. You wait for items in your future box to happen.

I cannot take credit for this technique. I've learned it through years of reading, studying, and talking to people, and this is a technique I first heard about browsing online. I added a few of my concepts to it, and this version of the three-box technique has benefited me. Hopefully, you can take it and customize it to your needs, and I believe it will be conducive to you. The key points to remember from this are that you have to be in a calm state and you have to be willing to think about the things that are bothering you. You must be able to identify where one issue begins and where it ends, not mix it or merge it with other problems, and then can objectively say that this goes in the past, present, or future box. Truthfully, the first time I did this, when it worked for me, I felt ridiculous because it made me wonder why I was so worried. I had nothing in my present box the first time I used this technique. The first few times I did this, I had nothing in my present box. Being able to categorize your stressors is all about just being able to converse with yourself. Instead of being angry about stuff, you need to be able to say that this thing is bothering me, this other thing is bothering me, I worry about this thing happening to me, I'm upset that this thing happened to me, etc. Once you can do that, you will find a quiet freedom in your mind and an incredible burden lifted off your shoulders.

Letting Go

When people look for a way to overcome sadness, anxiety, anger, or other issues, the suggestion that seems to be most common is that if you are happier, you must be able to let go. These two words, put together, seem very simple but have very complex roots. If we were to look at the words literally, the idea of letting something go means you are no longer holding onto it. So, does letting go mean not holding on to something? It has been my experience that many pieces of advice hinge on simply letting go. If you are under much stress, you should let it go. If something wrong or dramatic happens to you, if you keep thinking about that, you should just let it go. Nevertheless, what does it mean to let go?

What I find fascinating about this topic is the multitude of interpretations of 'letting go'. If you were to ask a group of people what it means, you would likely receive various answers. This diversity of perspectives not only enlightens us but also opens our minds to the complexity of this concept. It is not just that people describe the same thing differently, but it is as if 'letting go' has many different roots. It is not just about the various ways to let go, but the idea of what it means to let go can have a variety of origins. If letting go means many different things, then the act can be done in even more different ways.

Let's look at the concept of letting go in different cultures. This concept is perceived differently from a cultural perspective. In Latin American cultures, letting go has been frequently associated with Dia de los Muertos, the day of the dead. This version of letting go is about honoring those we have lost and helping those still here overcome that loss to move on. In this culture, letting go is all about life and death. It would be best if you let go of the grief and the sadness of losing that person, and once you do, then you can move forward with living a fuller life yourself. It is not about forgetting people but about remembering them and honoring them in a productive way that allows you to move forward (DeHaas, 2105). It focuses more on the memory of the person and less on the sadness of not being here. From this perspective, letting go may be seen as letting go of loss so you can gain more from life.

In indigenous cultures, letting go is closely tied to community and nature. There are many ceremonies and rituals for letting go, such as the 'smudging' ceremony in Native American culture, which involves burning sacred herbs to cleanse a space or person (Bayley, 2017). These practices are closely tied with storytelling, remembering past events, and genuinely focusing on the connections between people in the natural world. Like Latin American culture, it does have a connection with death, but it also has to do with letting go of past events. From this perspective, letting go can be seen as a sign of forgiveness or a way to move forward from unfortunate events.

Another form of communal togetherness is the concept of 'letting go' in African cultures. They celebrate the 'Ubuntu' concept, meaning "I am because we are" (DePetris, 2023). This is yet another example of togetherness and community. This idea is deeply ingrained in the notion of community support. The individual is meant to help the community. The individuals themselves will never be as successful as those in a group. These groups get together and help the individuals move forward and let go of individual struggles. They can only heal and move forward as a unit by having the individuals work together in a community. This emphasis on community and support makes us feel connected and supported in our journey of 'letting go'.

Letting go refers to working together in a communal matter. In some cultures, such as the Middle Eastern cultures, letting go can be associated with the concept of "Tawakkul," which means to put trust in God's Plan (Jamil, 2022). This ideology encourages people to overcome their fears, stresses, and worries. Put your trust in God and divine wisdom. People should not worry about what happens because everything happens for a reason. In this idea of letting go, we are not looking at things from a communal perspective or working together as a group. We are letting go of what bothers us and believing that we are better served by our belief in a higher power rather than understanding why something we perceive as unfavorable has happened.

This idea of letting go because we have no control is associated with Middle Eastern cultures and the Eastern cultures of Buddhism and Taoism, which also have a solid connection to this concept. In Buddhism, letting go is associated with not having an attachment. Letting go could be associated with not having an attachment to material possessions and desires, which leads to suffering. Embracing this idea of attachment and only needing what is necessary is used to help achieve inner peace and enlightenment. In Buddhism, letting go is letting go of the things you do not have to and embracing yourself. Taoism is similar but has some distinct differences. Letting go aligns with the "wu wei" principle, which means not exerting oneself or effortless action (Reninger, 2019). This principle is based on the idea that people should not fight what happened to them but let go and flow with the natural course of actions in life. Do not fight or resist the things that happen. Let go of control and go with the Tao (The Way). The element of water is typically used to depict this belief because water will flow. This idea is one of Bruce Lee's teachings. A famous quote about this belief is, "Be Water, My Friend". In this quote, he says, "Be like water making its way through cracks. Do not be assertive, but adjust to the object, and you shall find a way around or through it. If nothing within you stays rigid, outward things will disclose themselves. Empty your mind, be formless. Shapeless, like water. If you put water into a cup, it becomes the cup. You put water into a bottle, and it becomes the bottle. You put it in a teapot. It becomes the teapot. Now, water can flow, or it can crash. Be water, my friend. (Neill, 2011)"

Western culture and its perspective on letting go seem to take concepts from other cultures. However, they are more centralized on the individual. The belief and active letting go are specifically focused on individual growth and self-improvement. It is about learning from the past, pushing forward, and not fighting change. Western culture associates letting go of mental health. Negative thoughts are released, and the positive is embraced.

Because letting go is not a firm principle but more of a belief, it can differ significantly from culture to culture. How we perform this act will be very different based on our mindset. We should look at letting go and believing in one culture more than the other, or we should look at letting go and people having different issues that they need to let go of.

The Latin American culture focuses more on death, whereas the indigenous and African cultures focus more on community. Middle Eastern culture addresses letting go as letting go of some events because they are part of God's plan. Buddhism focuses on letting go of the material devices in life and delusions that impact how we see day-to-day life. In contrast, Taoism, for lack of a better term, tells you to go with the flow by releasing resistance and control again. Western culture tells us that we need to grow individually by letting go of those negative thoughts because they are harming us and not allowing us to focus on a healthier state of mind.

I believe that letting go is good advice; however, understanding your problem is more critical than simply letting go of it. Many of the books and writings that I read about this topic suggest letting go as a solution for dealing with stress and anxiety but don't consider what the problem is and how different problems may require different styles of letting go. My goal is to let you know what works for me, and in this case, the concept of letting go is not something that could be done at this stage, and this is where I made one of my more significant mistakes. I didn't realize until years into it that I first understood my problem. What led to my stress and anxiety? What was it that would make me depressed and even get me to the point where I started thinking about how to get over these issues? What seems very simple now, but I didn't understand that was that I couldn't solve the issue of how I felt. I needed to solve the issue of what led to how I felt. In my mind, everything is a series of causes and effects. The effects were what led me to be anxious and overwhelmed. It's the cause that I needed to delve into and understand.

I needed to have a better understanding of what led to these symptoms. What was my problem? I had a lot of problems. I had a lot of issues that I was contending with, and they each had their resulting stressor. A person needs to identify each issue, and you can find a solution. But the key to this is twofold. First, you have to solve the cause, not the effect. You must focus on the issue, not how you feel. Second, we can only solve one problem at a time.

It seems like a lot of common sense, it may be, but it wasn't very apparent right away. It was especially unclear to me how many layers there were in these thoughts and problems. In the end,

16

what made it more feasible for me was the need to identify each stressor and then identify the problem that led to that stressor. Furthermore, although some problems were interlaced, I had to deal with them individually. In the end, I realized that I needed to solve the cause of my problems and address them individually.

This is where letting go becomes essential. As you see, there may be some commonalities in how different cultures see the concept of letting go. However, there certainly are a lot of differences. Letting go seems to simply be an idea, regardless of the culture, that each type of problem has a solution. I identified my different problems and understood that there were different definitions of letting go, which worked together so that, depending on my problem, I could look at the different techniques each culture subscribed to and see which one was related to my issue. For example, if it was due to a loss where a friend or family member passed away, I took more of the Latin American perspective, knowing that I would be better served moving forward with the memory of the person rather than constantly thinking about what I had lost. If it's an issue where something negative was happening but I had no control over it, such as my favorite sports team not winning, a power tool that burnt out, a downed tree from a significant storm, etc. I would look at it from the Taoism perspective, and we just have to go with the flow. There's nothing they could do when looking back; all you can do is try to be flexible about the damage that was done and work toward a solution. If there was a problem where there was a burglary or a fire in someone's house was destroyed, I imagine the African perspective of coming together as a community would probably be the most effective way to deal with it. The key is to identify the problem and how to address it. It's important to remember that none of these solutions have the illusion of thinking that you are in control. Some of these concepts may not work for you. For example, suppose you're not a religious person. In that case, feeling as though something negative that happened is an act of God is not going to be a reassuring thought. It doesn't matter. There is an answer to every problem. Based on what happened to you, it may be more beneficial to look at it as a problem, accept it, and move forward.

If nothing is held onto and we all let go of issues as they occur, what kind of life would that be? We would have memories; we would be upset about things that happened in the past and happy about things that happened in the past. We would also look forward to things in the future or perhaps dread items that have yet to come. If we did this and let go, we would be left with feelings. However, we didn't focus our time dwelling on those events to the point where they occupied our lives; what would be left with is another buzzword we hear all the time: living in the moment. If we truly let go, our minds not focused on the future or the past, and we lived in the present and asked about things that occurred as we experienced that event, we would not only be able to enjoy that more, but we would be able to focus more on ourselves and our minds to what was going on at that exact moment.

So far, we've discussed not dwelling in the past or dreading the future but living in the present. Not only would this help us reduce stressors and anxiety, but it would also allow us to put all of our energy into the things that we were doing at that moment. Therefore, letting go is not just something to help us move forward; it will allow us to live in the moment and enjoy life more by focusing entirely on what we are doing. We wouldn't have our mind elsewhere stewing about how someone in a grocery store skipped ahead of us in line or how we have a meeting at work tomorrow with a coworker we don't like. These things don't matter.

Once it has already happened, nothing you do will make it any better. In the meeting example, it hasn't even happened yet. Maybe it'll go well or be as frustrating as it has been in the past, but you'll be OK, just as you have always been. Let those go and focus entirely on what you are doing now. You may be with your child or spouse or just driving and listening to music. With your mind free of stress, that moment can be fully immersed in what you are doing.

Cause and Effect

The concept of cause and effect seems extremely simple and is understood by many people; however, its practice and how it applies to different aspects of life is only sometimes applied. I always think of Newton's cradle with this concept. People react to the metal ball that swings into the air, but the first ball swinging into the group causes the effect. A concept I will keep referring to is that people tend to realize there is an issue or get upset or have anxiety due to what they would consider to be a problem. In the context of cause and effect, they react to an "effect". Naturally, they want to solve this problem, so they will look at the problem or "effect" and attempt to rectify it. The "effect" is not the problem but a result of the problem; they need to address the "cause." By identifying the cause, we identify the trigger which led to the problem. You've probably heard of this as getting to the root of a problem, presenting it as cause and effect, is easier for me because it's simpler to visualize that an action leads to an event.

Again, most people know this, but it is only sometimes applied. In business, project managers and industry leaders constantly examine how a product or initiative failed to correct itself for the next iteration. This is done by performing an after-action report or root cause analysis. An exercise like this aims to delve deep into a project and identify where something went wrong or why it could have been more successful than expected. This concept can be applied to any part of a business.

In our everyday lives, the cause-and-effect problem is evident in many other ways. For example, you may have frequent arguments with your significant other, and if you were to explain this to your friends, you might say, "We just argue all the time". There is no solution to a generic argument. In this case, the argument would be the "effect", and the reason or type of argument would be the "cause". Some of the more common types of problems may include general communication issues, where the cause would be that due to a lack of effective communication or misunderstanding, an issue would lead to regular arguments and frustration. The issues originate from a lack of trust. Perhaps there was a previous history of betrayal or infidelity now, the effect of which is the lack of trust and suspicion of where your significant other is and what they're doing. Many problems stem from differing values. This may be as simple as a Republican versus Democrat or a different viewpoint. Still, because of differing beliefs, the effect (i.e., religion, immigration laws, raising a child, etc.) of this could be a recurring argument about that topic. Not only will this argument keep coming up, but it may never get resolved if you have fundamentally opposing views.

Understanding and recognizing cause and effect is essential to addressing problems from this dynamic. An important aspect of this concept is identifying the cause (i.e., trigger) and understanding how that will lead to arguments or conflicts, which then lead to stress and anxiety. Another aspect of cause and effect is to resolve the causal issue because it just comes back if it's not resolved. The bare minimum of the problem is that there will be an argument, but that's only the beginning point. The argument will then begin to grow, and if there are other variables at play, such as you have been drinking or are impaired, have had other problems that day, etc., the argument can then exponentially escalate and even lead to violence. When you look back on the situation, the cause of the problem is not violent behavior; it's not how you reacted to the argument.

How do we stop these problems? When the cause of a problem is identified, it needs to be resolved. People who leave their issues unresolved or "agree to disagree" may notice that the problem can fester and recur each time, becoming more significant. If the problem can't be resolved, the next best option is to identify the cause or trigger and stop the conversation at that point. One common technique is using a safe word or simply identifying the problem, saying we should not continue this conversation because it never ends well.

Self-reflection is critical when it comes to this topic. It would help find the topics that cause you stress and identify what leads to the escalation. If you feel constantly stressed when you have a project at work, you should prepare your projects earlier so that there is not so much pressure. Some people lean more towards getting an extension and asking for help, but those are secondary issues. The real issue is how you feel and what makes you feel pressure. Another technique is to analyze your root causes, and we consistently ask why. Why am I upset? Why is this happening? Why do I react this way? It may seem childish, but you will drill down to its roots by consistently asking why. This will require you to investigate yourself and identify common traits or patterns.

You may notice that a typical pattern might be involved when you consistently react a certain way. It's also incumbent on you to take care of yourself. If you find that these problems, for example, with work, keep coming up repeatedly, you might need to ask if you're doing the correct type of job. It could be the job that is an issue or a manager or corporate belief. Suppose you tend to feel this way regularly in a relationship. In that case, you should evaluate yourself more than your partner and identify whether you consistently engage in relationships with people with specific traits. Your quality of life is of paramount importance. Your mental health is more important than your salary or the person you are with. In both these cases and many others, being happier and being with something or someone not considered ideal by societal standards will lead to an overall happier scenario. Would you instead earn 20% less in a job where you are far happier? Perhaps you don't date someone who expects you to make a specific salary or live a higher lifestyle rather than someone who accepts you for who you are.

These concepts stem from a cause-and-effect model where something happens, leading to a situation where problems form. Our goal is to look inward and understand that the real problem is us not recognizing the initial issue and resolving it. By letting the initial issue or "cause" go unresolved, we open ourselves up to the "effect," which puts us in a delicate situation where the problems originate from and lead to potentially dangerous confrontations. We have the right and ability to regulate what we get upset with, and we have the responsibility to ourselves to identify these triggers and stop them before we allow ourselves to hurt ourselves.

Never Worry

I was too afraid to have my life flash before my eyes because I was too busy splashing and looking for help. For the second time in my life, I nearly drowned in this natural quarry that was about 80 feet deep. When I was 15 years old, I was floating on the water on a little raft, and I got out around to go to a rock ledge to see the kids jumping into the water. I decided to jump in as well, but I would do it near my raft, and then I would get in my raft and continue floating around as I had been that hot summer afternoon. My plan didn't work as I expected. I jumped off the ledge and splashed just a foot away from my raft. Unfortunately, I didn't think about this before diving into the water. As you can imagine, the waves from my splash pushed my raft further away. With each wild stroke I took, I was causing other little splashes and pushing my raft further and further away. Before long, I had a horrible cramp and started to sink. Thankfully, a lifeguard was watching, and they jumped in and saved me. It's a shame I didn't learn my lesson that day.

July 8, 2023, I was swimming at the same quarry when I got a cramp and began to panic. I didn't know it at the time, but months later, I learned that I had a pinched nerve in my neck, which would cause my arm to lock up on me and seize. I was swimming in the quarry with my family. Some had life vests on rafts or giant logs that people would try to sit or stand on. Suddenly, my arm locked up, and I cramped up. Once again, I tried to save myself and swim back to my raft, but I couldn't mentally do it, and physically, I suffered for it. The combination of this happening for a second time here resulted in vivid flashbacks. In addition, those flashbacks of the drowning are also purely reminiscent of a panic attack. You don't want to have these two thoughts simultaneously, especially why you're sinking in water. My wife and kids surrounded me, and I don't think they realized it was as bad as I thought it was because most of it was probably in my head. However, I would've been entirely underwater and sinking if another few seconds had passed. So, for a second time, I had a lifeguard jump in and save me in the same quarry. Even when we got out of the water, I was still in the midst of another panic attack.

In my head, for the second time in my life, I thought I was going to die. I know I had only begun to go underwater, combined with the other events, which made this one of my life's scariest times. I wouldn't consider this a near-death experience, but I do look at it as one of the most important events of my life. Once I finally settled down, I had a feeling wash over me the way the water had in the quarry. I felt like nothing mattered, and the only important thing was my loved ones. For days, I felt appreciation and gratitude for being alive. Things that would've upset me didn't bother me because everything seemed insignificant.

For days after this event, nothing could bother me. My food tasted better, everything smelled better, and I was so happy to be alive. But a couple of weeks went by, and this feeling subsided. I began to get frustrated with things, and anxiety and worry began to settle back in. I decided I wanted to remember that feeling all the time. I got a tattoo that represents drowning, which I have no choice but to look at every day with the hope that I will hold onto that feeling and have a stronger appreciation every day. It's ironic, but remembering that terrifying experience helps me appreciate the experiences even to this day and remember what is truly important. If I earned anything that day, it is always to be appreciative. It's so cliche to say things like carpe diem each day like your last, and there are countless songs about this. I can't speak for other people, but I never lived that way until I had this experience. Take my advice on this mindset and appreciate each day like it's your last, and don't wait until you nearly die to know this is a better way to live. In case you're wondering, I won't swim there anymore.

It has also led me to study anxiety, which leads to worry and I try not to get to a point where I can dismiss what could lead to worrying by using the three-box technique. I understand where worrying comes from, when it should be discarded as something that happened, and when it should be something you focus on. Most things that lead to worrying correlate with the three boxes, but it led me on a mission to combat worrying. Then, in most scenarios, it is dismissed as a useless emotion that is good for nothing.

Worrying is entirely counterproductive, terrible for you, and unnecessary. However, the more significant message is that we must learn our minds better and understand what we think and feel. When we feel overwhelmed, have a great deal in our minds, and are concerned, we tend to think of it all as worrying. We have multiple thoughts that can be seen as events and issues.

Let's consider the topics that people worry the most about. The biggest worry for most people is financial instability, instability of the future, pandemics, global warming, natural disasters, food shortages/famine, clean water, nuclear weapons, cyber-attacks, worsening air quality, and the role of artificial intelligence. These are some of the topics I found from my recent study that I read and topics I've seen on other sites and studies. These are the items that caused the most worry. Review the list and look at it from the perspective of events and issues. You can see how these items fall into one of these two categories and how there's far less to worry about, you may realize.

I process data when I break it down to its most simplistic form. I like to define events and issues based on whether we can do something about them. An event is something potentially negative that may happen, but you can't do anything about it. For instance, a natural disaster is an event. There is a distinct difference between issues and events. An issue is something potentially negative that has happened, and something can be done about it. You have no control over an event, and an issue is a problem you must solve. If you were to review that list again of the top items people worry about with this mindset, you would see many would-be events. At the same time, only a few would be issues unless it has occurred and directly impacted you.

Financial security is tricky because, theoretically, you can do something about it. We could try to improve ourselves, get degrees or training to get a better job, get a side job, and perhaps cut down on some of our expenses; therefore, with this mindset, we could say financial security is an issue and is something we need to worry about. Cyber security threats, and, for that matter, other technical-related matters, could be seen as an issue as well. You can't control if someone tries to hack or steal your information. However, it is your responsibility to exercise caution and protect yourself online to a degree. In short, you can do something to lessen the severity of this, and because you have control over how much this affects you, this is an issue.

Following this line of thinking, it might be feasible to say that all the other items are events. You may disagree with your personal history and beliefs. However, in my perspective, I see them as events in the sense that they haven't happened yet, and when they do happen, you will address them. Another way to look at it is that you must control it for it. You have no control over whether there's another pandemic. You have no control over whether there'll be another war. The only thing you have control over is how you react to it when it occurs; that is when it becomes an issue or a problem.

The chapter on the three boxes discusses the past, present, and future boxes. An event would go in our future box. It has yet to happen, so it's not a problem for you. I'm not saying that the items listed are not horrible things. If they do occur, typically, there's a lot of negativity and issues that come along with it. My point is that we should not treat something that may or may not happen at a future date the same as an actual problem you are facing. Therefore, the items are events and may happen at a future date. When they happen, they will have their dynamic circumstances surrounding them and are not something to worry about. They may be something to be sad about, or they may be sad, but it is not the same as a problem that you're presently facing.

An example of how these events and issues differ from the other point of view is to look at a natural disaster. Some parts of the United States are prone to hurricanes, and others are prone to tornadoes. Some parts of the world are prone to different kinds of disasters. This event will probably occur, but you need to know when, and you don't know the details or its degree of severity. You cannot do anything to prevent this. You can only help put yourself in the best possible situation to minimize the damage if you happen a little in these areas. Therefore, taking these protective measures becomes part of your life. You may take out a specific type of insurance, for there's a bunker built for some other protective measure to help you when this disaster occurs. It's not a consistent issue because once you have taken these measures, you simply wait for that natural disaster. Suppose you have financial concerns about how to pay a bill at the end of the month. In that case, it is not only a recurring issue every month, but it is expected and has an actual due date. This is something that impacts your day-to-day life. You may decide whether to make certain purchases, so you have more money to make these payments. On the one hand, as it relates to the natural disaster, you may take some protective measures and hope for the best; on the other hand, when it pertains to financial stability, every time you make a financial purchase, the stock is in your mind, and it is a more prevalent issue.

Let's look at what worries us in this framework of events and issues. Events are something in our mind that we will deal with when they occur, and we may take some preventative measures to reduce their impact. Issues are prevalent problems, and we can solve them one at a time if there is a solution. I have found that there are only a few actual issues at any given time. Suppose you relegate worrying to only issues and discard events as potentially unfortunate. However, you won't put much effort into it until it happens. In that case, you'll find a much more accessible mind that is free from worry.

This concept of issues and events ties into the three-box technique in the sense that your issues, which are your problems, would go in your present box, and your events, which may happen at some point in the future, would go in your future box. These techniques work together, but they are like subsets of one another. There's nothing wrong with being prepared and thinking about the future. However, what is wrong is to worry about these things consistently. Excessive worrying, which originates with stress and anxiety, is not only something that will cause you to be very depressed, but it is detrimental to your overall health. Heart disease, high blood pressure, hypertension, and strokes are just some of the issues that you could bring on yourself from worry, which leads to stress and anxiety.

As with many things, it goes into a downward spiral that accelerates its damage. Trying to be proactive and thinking about all the things that could happen, you may leave yourself to worry too much, and then when you do, you're going to have more stress and more anxiety. When you do, your problems will compound, and you will have a variety of answers to solve the problems. The thoughts and concerns will consume you and begin to impact your day-to-day life, your ability to sleep, and your outlook on life. It will begin to impact your relationships. Each of these things causes significantly more stress and anxiety, which would then cause more damage to you by then, leading to some of the health problems we listed. Once again, anytime you have problems, they can only be solved on a case-by-case basis. You can only solve one problem at a time. When you get into these downward spirals, problems exponentially increase. This makes it considerably more challenging to resolve these issues; however, there is a more straightforward solution. They can free you from significant burdens. Keep the idea of events and issues in the forefront of your mind, and when things come up, is this a problem that you need to solve, or is it something potentially harmful that may occur in the future? You only need to carry the issues with you. The events affect all of us. There is no reason for you to carry its weight.

Everything is Temporary

    Try to imagine the happiest moment of your life. It's hard for many people to do because, hopefully, you've had many great memories. So, instead, try to imagine the most horrible moment of your life. Again, a specific event may only come to mind after some thought. Whatever your most fantastic or worst memories are, the most important thing about them is that they have ended. Someone may meet the love of their life and see their wedding day as the perfect day, and then, a couple of years later, they get divorced and think that that person is one of the worst creatures that ever walked on the Earth. Everything is temporary, and nothing is permanent. No matter how great or horrible an event is, it will end. One of the most important sayings that lends itself to this concept is "This too shall pass." There are several arguments over where this saying originated from. The theory that comes up the most is that it comes from Persian Sufi poets. This, too shall pass, is translated to "in nīz bogzarad," which refers to the impermanent nature of the human condition and how the ups and downs we all experience in life will pass (Mashburn, 2024).

    Where this saying originated from is less important than what it means. If you take a step back and think about it, everything that starts will come to an end. Some people could get philosophical about this and look at it regarding life's beginning and ending. I prefer to think of it in a much more simplistic manner. Every event will eventually finish and become a memory, and it's worth remembering. If I stubbed my toe on the corner of my bed, it would hurt, but it would end. If I have a phenomenal meal, the excellent taste will soon disappear. My memory of how good it tastes may also disappear, or maybe I'll think of it occasionally when I eat that type of meal again.

If we think about how we react to fantastic news and how we react to horrible news, it could have a significant emotional impact. Should we let this happen to us? Should we let the most fantastic news or a significant accomplishment make us happy, knowing it will end? Should we let terrible news make us extremely sad? Knowing those emotions will leave us, I feel sadness and relief. Of course, we should undoubtedly feel emotion, happiness, and sadness. We are human beings. There is no reason that we shouldn't feel. We should avoid mixing having an emotional reaction with holding onto an event, as that would never end.

Having your first love come to an end and having your first break up is something that naturally leaves us very sad. The person you had a deep relationship with, maybe even loved, is no longer in your life. You may feel rejected and feel that nobody will ever want you again. These are all emotional reactions. Typically, putting someone in that situation will also make them feel they'll never get over it again. At that point, someone in a similar situation will try to console them and explain how they will get over this and how there will be others in their life that they'll love. For example, parents may see that their son or daughter has had their first significant breakup and will try to help explain that this feeling will pass. They understand because they've been through it before. They know that their child is in pain, but this feeling is temporary and it's not permanent.

How we should see ourselves pertains to the techniques and concepts we've been discussing, especially the three boxes technique discussed earlier and its positive effects. When something happens, it is an event. However, the event leads to reactions to that event, and an event is a temporary occurrence. This is simply something that happened. Even if the impact of this alters our life, its emotions must be seen as a temporary event so that you can move forward.

One such example for me was when I got my master's degree. I was thrilled and incredibly proud of myself, seeing it as a significant accomplishment. However, it quickly dawned on me that all I had done was complete a portion of my schooling. I certainly was very proud of what I had done. However, I couldn't spend the rest of my life saying I've got this degree, but I knew it was a milestone in my greater academic goal of earning my doctorate.

The next day, I started looking for schools I could enroll in toward my Ph.D. It took me two weeks to find a program, which was very grueling because I felt like I was wasting time. I wouldn't let myself sit in that mode and be complacent because I knew I had to keep pushing forward and stay focused. Ironically, when I got my PhD, I was very proud, but within short order, that familiar thought came back to me: What will you do now?   Each of these events was something. I was proud of this accomplishment, but it didn't define me. It didn't make me any different than anyone else. I liked being called "Dr. Z", but not as a status symbol. It sounded cool, like a villain from a James Bond novel.

I remember the first time I started teaching upper-level classes where the instructors were all PhDs. I introduced myself to one of my colleagues, a fellow instructor, and I introduced myself by my first name and told him the classes I would be teaching. He referred to himself as Dr. Such and such. I chuckled because I thought he was joking and being overly formal. I referred to him by his first name. He looked at me sternly and said I earned this degree and this title, which is how everybody will refer to me. I lost a ton of respect for that man right there. Just because he had an accomplishment allowed it to define himself. It was the most crucial thing in his life, which is sad. I will always remember when I was a student in my graduate program, I had a conversation with an instructor who was more like a mentor to me. He told me I should not get a big head when I graduate and get a doctorate. Earning a Ph.D. doesn't change who you are or how important you are. He had seen many peers forget that lesson and wanted to stress it to future graduates.

Even earning that degree is just another event. Sure, Dr. Such and Such and I finished an academic goal, but it doesn't make you better than other people. It's like being an accountant or a lawyer. Because you've been certified in a topic or meet the need for a specific title, you can perform some professional activities. The title is just a representation of that certification, and students referring to you that way is a matter of respect; insisting other people refer to you by a title outside of that setting is a sign of insecurity. It doesn't mean that it changed the rest of your life because you were able to graduate. It just means that it is a part of who you are.

Another example of this, which I feel is far more impressive, is that I knew a gentleman growing up whom this book referred to as Tom. Tom was a coworker of mine at a college and was a fantastic teacher. I worked with him for years; he had the best reviews and respect from his peers and students.   Years later, I went to work as a security analyst. As soon as I could start making recommendations, one of the people recommended we hire him for our group. He consistently worked towards building new systems and developing database solutions that would expedite what we did. He would come in early and stay late and had more pride in his work than anyone I've ever met. Although he was in his 60s at this point in his life, when he was 16 years old, he went swimming in Chesapeake Bay and into a shallow portion of the bay. His head hit the bay floor and broke his neck. From that point on, Tom had quadriplegia.

He would get to and from work, sometimes from his wife in their wheelchair-accessible van and other times from a state mobility service that would pick him up and drop him off at work. I'm sure many mobility employees are great at their jobs. However, some of the workers of this service didn't treat their passengers with the care they deserved, and the passengers weren't properly secured in their seats. On one occasion, from not being secured in his seat and the poor driving, Tom's thumb broke, but he stayed upbeat, saying something he couldn't feel, so it is what it is. Years later, the thumb healed. On another occasion, he broke both bones in his leg (tibia and fibula), which was never operated on because it could cause other issues. With Tom's incredible humor, he says he'll just refrain from dancing.

There were days when it would take him several hours to get to and from work. I don't think Tom ever complained about a thing. Occasionally, he would ask someone to get him a coffee. Tom didn't use highly advanced technology to assist his work. He had a metal rod with a mouthguard and a rubber-like cap on the other side. He would use that to push the keys on the keyboard, and that's how he typed.   Although, technically, Tom had quadriplegia, he had minimal movement in his arms, and that was how he would control the mouse.

Tom treated what happened in the past as an event that changed his life. After years in different hospitals and medical facilities, he started working, and from then on, he lived in that situation. He didn't carry the anger around because he knew it wouldn't serve any purpose. Living in that way just became his new norm. Those of us who worked with him loved him. If Tom liked you enough to let you get him a coffee or feed him a snack, you didn't consider it a burden but an honor.

Terrific things and horrible things happen all the time. We need to react to them appropriately, which becomes another life event. From the perspective of the three boxes, it would go into the past box. It was just one thing that happened. Whether it became a memory or if your life was different moving forward, it just became the new normal. Whether it was my doctorate or Tom's paralysis, once that situation had run its course, you would put your feelings for it aside and move forward. My life is the same with a doctorate as it would have been without it because I didn't expect people to treat me differently. You can have a positive or negative event, but it's just an event, and whether it changes your life or not, you adapt to the norm and move forward. We don't carry the successes and failures of our lives as the main emphasis of who we are. Who we are becomes the emphasis of our lives.

In my case, it meant I had finished the academic program and had more professional credibility. In Tom's situation, the broken neck became an event, and he learned how to live with that injury. Once He didn't carry that anger, he adjusted his life to a new norm. Spending those years working with Tom and getting to know him was an event where I let my emotions subside. However, it changed me mentally, and I understood what strength is, that everything is temporary, and that what we choose to react to is up to us.

From a far less excessive perspective, if you're driving down the street and somebody cuts you off, we all know people who get upset that someone not only cut them off but potentially endangered them and could cause an accident. At that point, the event ends, and the cycle ends, where the occurrence is temporary. The people who hold onto that anger continue to yell and scream, honk the horn, speed up, and try to cut that person off or engage in some form of road rage, which we want to avoid. Once that person had cut you off, it was over. By becoming aggressive, you are now actively starting a new event. Some people may argue that they were continuing the event. However, you are essentially lobbying back that ball of anger anytime you retaliate.

We need to see everything as a temporary event. Everything in life is temporary; the only difference is whether its effect is long-term or not. Is this event's impact something you could move on from, or does it require you to establish a new baseline and redefine what normal means to you?

Do it Right the First Time

We all know we should do the right thing, but perhaps doing things right is equally important. For various reasons, if you do anything, whether cutting the grass, taking out the trash, building a shed, painting a room, or any task, no matter how big or small, you want to do it as well as you possibly can. You were taught this lesson even as a child, but the reasons for doing it are sometimes lost. Yes, there is a degree of respect for your work and integrity in what you do. We certainly want to do an excellent job because we don't want people to look down on us. We also want to do an excellent job because we should have integrity and pride. Aside from that, other reasons are more self-serving. We all have a reputation to uphold, and we don't want to be seen as someone who cuts corners. These are credible reasons, but I have a rather unusual perspective for why we want to do an excellent job on each task.

No matter what, when you perform a task, you only do that one thing when doing the task. That means you're not doing anything else. For example, if you are doing something as simple as raking the leaves, the time you're spending on that task, you are doing something other than the countless things that can be done on Earth. You are sacrificing the ability to do everything else except for that one task of raking leaves. Since you're foregoing the act of doing anything else ever conceived by a human so that you could do this one task, you may want to focus on that task and do it as well as you can.

There is a reputation and a degree of pride in your work. However, selfishly, if you don't do the task well again, returning to our example of raking leaves, you will have to do that task again. Considering it from the broader perspective, you are not doing anything else. The only thing worse than having to do something and nothing else would be to do a poor job and have to do that same task again. Once again, you are doing a singular task that prevents you from doing anything else. Suppose you are doing a single task for a second time, and it prevents you from doing anything else. In that case, it seems ridiculous that you wouldn't just take the time to do it correctly the first time. Your time is valuable to you. Taking the time to do something and focusing on that one task and nothing else is far more critical than many people realize.

Your time may be the most valuable commodity in your life, even more than health. We all live a life that will come to an end, and we don't know when it will come to an end. So, imagine your life is like a countdown running in the background, and every second that passes is a second you can't get back. You're taking the time to perform tasks that preclude you from doing anything else and then decide not to give it your entire focus. Then, you must go back again to do that task, which precludes you from doing anything else while having the precious seconds of your life ticking away. To take this to an even higher level, the days that people who don't put their total effort into a task and must redo their tasks display this is a recurring behavior because, for one reason or another, they're looking for a reason to finish that task quicker. Suppose you begin to cut corners and not put your total effort into a task that becomes part of your core personality. You become a person who takes on the perspective of "good enough is good enough." Being average is just trying to do enough to get by. This may work in some cases, but in many cases, it will be incomplete and require you to do it again if you take the time to do a task and choose not to do anything else. We certainly don't want to repeat that task or develop the traits that will make this a recurring behavior where you do many tasks repeatedly.

I was a person who felt that "good enough is good enough". However, I have worked towards going away from that model and focusing on "doing it right the first time". This idea of it being a valuable aspect of my life and losing time is something that I realized later. The idea of taking pride in ownership and my work in the idea that my name was on something, so it needed to be done well, was a lesson I learned in the Army. If there was a singular event or lesson that made me begin to think about things this way, it was that when a very close family member of mine had a triple bypass, I began thinking about their life and if they were happy with the way things were. I didn't ever feel this person's life was in danger or that there was a significant chance that they wouldn't make it. Seeing the people in the cardiac wing of this hospital made this thought more ingrained in my thought process. Seeing men and women in their 70s and 80s openly talk to friends and family about how they wanted to make changes, they felt it was too late to make a significant change. They talked about wasting time and wishing they could do things over. Again, as years passed, I had a couple of minor health issues, nothing significant, but they still required medical attention. I would see people in waiting rooms and people in rehab centers who again had this conversation with their loved ones and, in some cases, with me while we were waiting to be seen. As you get older, you have milestone birthdays and begin reflecting on yourself even more. At this point, this lot became even more cemented in my mind because if I was going to take the time to do "a thing," I wanted to make sure that that "thing" was done right so that I wouldn't have to do it again. So, it wasn't any particular event. However, the combination of a military mindset, seeing other people go through health issues, having your health issues, and having milestone birthdays were all contributors to cementing this idea in my mind.

If there is a lesson to be taken from this, it is to look at things from a glorious perspective with a sense of finality and be macro in your vision. What I mean by that is that you should look at every second you have as a gift, and if you take those seconds to do something, you certainly want to use that gift wisely. Again, this is a selfish perspective because it's all about thinking about yourself and ensuring you have time for other things. It would be best if you did a good job whenever you do anything for many reasons, but people need to think about themselves. Knowing how this impacts me is sometimes a more substantial reason for doing something than others think of me. Both are important, but self-awareness can drive us to live efficiently, and we must do something right when we do something.

The Measuring Stick

The measuring stick is a concept of how hard we should work or when we're doing enough. Many years ago, I served in the United States Army, and I had a drill sergeant who, in only the way a drill sergeant can say it was, "Do not compare yourself to poop and say you look good." He used much more colorful language than poop, but the idea was based on how hard you should work, and it is from this quote that I follow today as part of the measuring stick technique. In a more relatable context, consider the measuring stick a personal yardstick, a standard you set to determine when you've done enough or need to push harder.

When I was in the Army, we had to run 2 miles, and we wanted to finish it in 15 minutes or less. We would try to complete the run in under 15 minutes as part of our training. I remember doing a battalion run when we would run with other batteries on a big run, and then we would meet as a group.   There would be people who would finish in 15 minutes and 30 seconds and much more. There would always be one or two brave souls who would say something. They may have exceeded 15 minutes, but they still finish much faster than many other people. That is where they don't compare themselves to poop and say I look good would come out. I've carried that with my entire life.

Doing good at something doesn't mean you did better than others you've compared yourself to. It means you have exceeded the standard. Someone being happy that they scored 80% on a test would upset me because 80% is a B minus. It's not an "A". I certainly don't believe that everyone must be a perfectionist, but simply doing better than the people you are with as opposed to doing better than what a standard is for two entirely different ideals. Imagine the greatest athletes of our time. They were all better than everyone at their high school. Then they went to college and were just one of the group. To be better than other people in college, they would have to work harder. The same thing applies to a higher level when you go to the next level as a professional athlete if you watch documentaries on some of the most successful athletes of all time, such as Kobe Bryant, Tom Brady, Mike Tyson, Bruce Lee, Arnold Schwarzenegger, etc. These are not people who are content with being good or very good. Being a professional athlete, making a giant salary, or even above average, these are typically people who are obsessed with being a champion. These individuals would never stop working even when they reached elite status. After they conquered one profession, they moved on to another and worked towards conquering that. They did not consider themselves successful simply because they were slightly better than their peers. They had to be the best. Most of them are more famous for their preparation for the games rather than the games themselves. They're more recognized for their work ethic rather than their performance. They keep pushing and pushing to find a new way to succeed or improve their skills and jobs. I am not saying that the purpose of this chapter is to try to be the very best at what you're doing but to try your best and improve. To be your best, excelling at trying your best is a way to challenge yourself consistently. It's not about being better than everyone else but about being the best version of yourself.

Professional athletes aside, this is a mindset that not everyone should have. Still, it is apparent throughout society that there is a hole in a heart or brain surgeon and how much they had to work to get to that level of surgery. That's far more than graduating medical school. Technical pioneers such as Steve Jobs, Elon Musk,

Bill Gates, Jeff Bezos, etc., all took perfecting their craft, technology, and being a good businessperson to a whole other level.

Even still taking this to a more personal level that would apply to the average individual would be to try to excel in everything you do and do it right the first time. For instance, if you wash dishes, ensure they are spotless; if you cut the grass, try to cut it as perfectly as possible. If you're going to cook a meal, do you want to try to make it as good as you can? These are things we do in life that we want to do as well as we can. Have pride in your work. Striving for excellence is not just about impressing others but about the personal satisfaction and pride of doing your best.

Suppose we try to push ourselves to do everything we do to the best of our ability. In that case, we will improve to some degree every time we do that act. We will continue to grow and improve, but we will also inspire and teach those around us. By constantly pushing ourselves to the next level, we will improve and challenge our lives; from a health and fitness perspective, if you did ten push-ups one day with perfect form and hopefully the next day, you could do 11. The goal is that with each day doing more than the minimum, we will continue to develop.   Eventually, you'll do 20, 30, or more push-ups daily. This is important because if we don't push ourselves to try our very best at each task we attempt, we will become stagnant, and then, as time passes, we will diminish, and our performance will decrease. More than the average, we will continue to grow longer and stave off our diminishment.

Growing up, whether from a coach, teacher, or parent, most people have heard that they don't care if a child or student is the best at something. They care if that child or student is trying their best. Do your best. It is a familiar saying many of us have heard. If what you're doing is not very good, but you tried your best, then the next time you do that task, you should be at least slightly better at it. The same lesson we learn as children is the same valuable lesson we should learn as adults. We always do our best and will continue to grow. In the academic field, they refer to someone who is never stagnant and pushes themselves to learn and stay abreast of new developments in a particular field as a lifelong learner. I believe it is essential for all of us to keep that same mindset with all aspects of our lives and not just be lifelong learners in our chosen fields and in anything that we pursue but take that concept of always trying to learn new things and applying it to always trying to do our best. Suppose we all engage in this philosophy, and we're surrounded by other people who engage in the same philosophy. In that case, we will push ourselves and each other. Look at people in the military, organized sports, or even people who take a health and fitness class together.

You will see people who are not competing with themselves but with each other. This type of healthy competition drives us to be the best we can be and for the group to be the best they can be. The fundamental concept of competition and teamwork leads to excellence. We should all try to do better than we did last time and encourage those around us, whether in the workplace, sports or with family. Self-improvement is the key to success. By improving our physical and mental abilities, we become more and more resilient as people. Having confidence in yourself also leads to believing in your ability to solve problems, which ties back to the three boxes technique, especially solving the problems in the "present box".

Your Body

They say that you were born with nothing, and you die with nothing. All the money and the material possessions you gain throughout your life are things you cannot take with you after you pass away. Although I agree with that idea, a significant portion is missing. What you have while you're alive is a concept that's not discussed. I don't mean money or physical possessions. The "things" we accrue throughout our lives are tangible possessions that can easily be lost. As we discussed with the Buddhist mindset all year, it's holding onto all those possessions that can dilute us.

We have something extraordinary to take care of - our bodies. So yes, it's true that you were born with nothing and you die with nothing, but the thing that you have between being born and dying is your body. It is a vessel that carries you through your entire existence. Considering that all other possessions can be destroyed, lost, stolen, etc., your body is yours.

Suppose we live in a world where when you turn 16 years old, you get a driver's license and a vehicle. You were told that this vehicle is yours and it's the only vehicle you're ever allowed to have. You could build it up, decorate it, paint it, upgrade it, and do whatever you'd like. Remember that it is your only vehicle and will deteriorate if you do not care for it. In fact, not only will it deteriorate, but if you don't care for it properly, it will break down and even get to a level where it's potentially irreparable. If this were the case, we'd treat our cars like gold. So why do we not treat our bodies even like gold? I do understand some people treat their bodies like gold, and some treat them like platinum or diamonds. Some of us treat our bodies wonderfully; unfortunately, many do not. As I've gotten older and I've dealt with a couple of minor health issues, I've taken in what I've seen at the various medical facilities I've been to. Anytime I go to a hospital to visit somebody or a nursing home, I see the people who were there. I see people who are not just aged, but some have aged in a body they did not care for as well as they should've. It not only made their life harder but took away their freedoms from them. It prevented them from enjoying many other beautiful things we could enjoy.

I've even seen grandparents or parents who couldn't play with their children not because of an injury they sustained but because their bodies are so broken down from years of neglect. Growing up the way I did and what was seen as a norm then, it was widespread for people to smoke cigarettes. I smoked cigarettes for 16 years, and then two days after my 41st birthday. I got tired going up a flight of stairs. Other elements started to impact me, getting short of breath at other times. However, it was this time when I was going up a flight of steps following one of my children, and I thought it dawned on me that it was time for smoking to stop. I had tried to stop in the past but failed.

I was heavily motivated by other family members to stop smoking because they had young children who had to deal with secondhand smoke, and it also smelled terrible. Then, restrictions were applied as to where you could smoke. I remember that some restaurants began to have rules for not smoking in their dining area by eliminating the smoking section. Bars and nightclubs soon followed suit, which we thought was crazy because smoking went together with drinking. Smokers had to stand outside to smoke, then noticed that there were specific open venues, such as college campuses and hospitals, where you couldn't smoke anywhere on the grounds, even outside. It's strange because even though all these things were happening, I saw it as a progression, but when I couldn't smoke in a casino in Las Vegas on a trip I had taken, it hit home. I remember thinking there was no place to smoke. Even then, I continued smoking for another year or so, trying to quit now and then, but I didn't have the right reason, so those attempts failed. But when I got tired of following my children up the stairs, I got the reason I needed. I needed the reason, which stems from selfish roots. I needed to quit to be healthier and see these children grow up. Once I made that decision, I never smoked again.

We need more selfishness. We need to think from the perspective of what is best for us. We need to think about ourselves and, more specifically, our bodies. Thinking about what is best for me is the most important gift you can give yourself and your loved ones. Do you want to be there and spend years with them? Do you want to be able to enjoy whatever time you can with them? From my perspective, I know that at some point in time, the younger generation must care for older people. Still, caring for someone because they are older and caring for someone because they are medically incapacitated due to an illness they brought onto themselves from negligence are two very different things. The person who eats horribly and treats their body with total disregard, and then winds up developing a variety of disorders or diseases from ingesting obscene amounts of unhealthy food is essentially not only showing disregard for themselves but disregard for the one that was going to have to help take care of them. I am not overly obsessed with health or someone with a scale measuring every ounce of my diet. I am talking about responsible eating, a candy bar or two. However, we keep it to Halloween, some celebrations, and a few events. Keep it as a treat. If you want to indulge occasionally, eat fast food, but maybe we should not do it multiple times daily. Go for a walk, do some cardio, and do a few things that would not only be considered healthy and a form of exercise but also help you, your environment, and nature. I enjoy it when my wife and I take our two dogs for a walk. It's not only a bit of exercise walking around our neighborhood. We are spending quality time together.

The key is that if we do not care for our bodies, they will break down, and then we will become limited. Eventually, you're missing out on events because of it, and you begin to be trapped by your body. We all know how horrible it feels when we're sick and how much we want to be better and be out and doing things. We don't want to be stuck in a bed, but when we are, all we want to do is be better and not be stuck in bed. If you've ever broken a bone, you can't do the thing you want to do. Imagine having a broken leg up to your hip for the rest of your life. You can't use the bathroom on your own, you can't shower alone, and you begin to get exhausted. You are just trying to do basic things. These are all avoidable, but your body begins to break down. These are similar limitations that your body puts on you.

We don't all need the perfect body, and I don't feel that's reasonable, but we can all have a healthy body. This originates from love, not necessarily for another person but for yourself. Do you want to love yourself enough to take care of one thing that is truly yours in this life: your body?

In addition, it distresses the maintenance of your body. I believe it's essential that we see the entire body. Many people feel that maintaining their body is done by cardio because of your heart or doing exercises to help your muscles. However, your body's most important muscle is easily neglected. Your brain is important because, depending on your philosophies, it essentially houses your mind. As we grow with technology, we have more and more distractions that prevent us from exercising our minds. Whether it be shown on your device or video games, although some argue that it is a form of mental exercise, it is limited to devices (cars and AI) that do tasks for us. Technology like this takes away from our thinking and exercising our minds. Reading books, learning about history, engaging in debates and exciting conversation, and strategic games (i.e., chess, card games, Yahtzee if you play with my wife) are all games that can challenge you mentally.

Thinking about things you don't typically think about is a good start. However, as we focus on our push-ups, walking, weights, diet, and all the other things, we should incorporate them to some degree. We also need to incorporate your mind. Recently I've taken up painting. None of my works are anything that you would confuse with professional artwork. I only do it for myself and because I'm being selfish. When I paint, it's almost like escaping the world and entering my mental space. I'm creating something and thinking about what I want to make. Unfortunately, in many cases, I'm thinking about how it didn't turn out how I wanted it, but it looks OK. This is something that I do to challenge myself mentally and take my mind and thought process to a place that I can only get to when I'm painting. The first step is to look at your body as your car, which you have for the rest of your life. Remember that our car has an engine, body, seats, etc., and our body has its muscles, heart, mind, etc. Take care of yourself so that you are not stuck on the side of the road while everyone else drives by.

Taking care of your body is just the last of these lessons, but these thoughts are interwoven and meant to work together. I hope the lessons shared in this handbook are helpful to you not only as independent ideals but also together. Life is complex with ever-changing variables, and you can't always treat every situation equally. We need consistent morals and ethics, but even when we face the same type of situation at different times, we must look at the details and understand that each situation is unique. These ideals I've shared with you are more like guidelines. They're not immutable facts or inflexible rules. Your perspective may need to adjust as situations change.

Some lessons came easily, while others were born through significant hardship. They have guided me in self-improvement. I hope you can learn from my mistakes, take some of these lessons, and apply them to your life. I know life was very different for a parent when they were the same age as their kids, and it's different for everyone based on how and where they grew up. As a result, there are a lot of experiences people may miss growing up and others they go through repeatedly. You may live a life where you may or may not learn some of these lessons. I hope this handbook will reinforce and teach you those lessons.

Perhaps the thoughts and lessons in this handbook are more for me, and by writing them down, I can understand them better. I often thought that a wise person learns from their mistakes, a wiser person learns from mistakes they see others make, and the wisest person learns from history and does not need to make or be a part of a mistake to learn from it.

At my point in this journey, there are two things I've learned, which I'll leave you with. Firstly, I've come to a point where I'm just beginning to apply some of the concepts I have learned in my everyday life. These are by no means all of your life lessons. Secondly, it is undeniable that I've made far more mistakes in my decision-making process than correct ones. It's the act of looking at yourself and trying to improve that shows you're on the right path. It's taken me this long to look at some of the events in my life and how they've shaped me, and I wanted to share a few of those with you.

References

Bayley, N. (2017). Learning About Smudging With Old Hands Of The Shoshone First Nation. https://destinationindigenous.ca/blog/smudging-101-with-old-hands-of-the-shoshone-first-nation/

DeHaas, P. (2105). Dia de los Muertos: Reflections on Love, Death & Letting Go. | elephant journal. https://www.elephantjournal.com/2015/10/dia-de-los-muertos-reflections-on-love-death-letting-go/

DePetris, M. (2023). Embracing Ubuntu: How Collective Growth and Joy Empowers. https://magsdepetris.com/blog/embracing-ubuntu-shared-joy/

Drolet, E. (n.d.). Letting Go—Salty Souls Experience. Retrieved November 15, 2024, from https://saltysoulsexperience.com/letting-go/

Eysenck, M., Payne, S., & Santos, R. (2006). Anxiety and depression: Past, present, and future events. Cognition & Emotion, 20(2), 274–294. https://doi.org/10.1080/02699930500220066

Frank, M. A. (2011). The Worry Box Technique. https://www.excelatlife.com/articles/worry.htm

Govindarajan, V. (2016). The Three Box Solution: A Strategy for Leading Innovation—Book—Faculty & Research—Harvard Business School. https://www.hbs.edu/faculty/Pages/item.aspx?num=50752

Grupe, D. W., & Nitschke, J. B. (2013). Uncertainty and anticipation in anxiety: An integrated neurobiological and psychological perspective. Nature Reviews Neuroscience, 14(7), 488–501. https://doi.org/10.1038/nrn3524

Jamil, H. (2022). The Year of Running, Rebirthing, & a Divine Kind of Relying – The Book Jacket. https://thebookjacket.com/2022/12/31/the-year-of-running-rebirthing-a-divine-kind-of-relying/

Neill, C. (2011). "Be water, my friend" Bruce Lee—Moving People to Action. https://conorneill.com/2011/02/18/be-water-my-friend-bruce-lee/

Reninger, E. (2019). What Is the Meaning of Wu Wei as a Taoist Concept? https://www.learnreligions.com/wu-wei-the-action-of-non-action-3183209

Mashburn, R. (2024). "This Too Shall Pass": History, Origin, and Bible Teaching—Bible Study. https://www.crosswalk.com/faith/bible-study/this-too-shall-pass.html

www.ingramcontent.com/pod-product-compliance
Lightning Source LLC
Chambersburg PA
CBHW070810120626
46557CB00002B/794